© Aladdin Books Ltd 2001

Designed and produced by
Aladdin Books Ltd
28 Percy Street
London W1P 0LD

First published in
Great Britain in 2001 by
Franklin Watts
96 Leonard Street
London EC2A 4XD

ISBN 0 7496 4122 3

Printed in Belgium

Editor
Bibby Whittaker

Literacy Consultant
Rosemary Chamberlin
Westminster Institute of Education,
Oxford Brookes University

Design
Flick, Book Design and Graphics

Picture Research
Brian Hunter Smart

Illustration
Mary Lonsdale for SGA

Picture Credits
Abbreviations: t – top, m – middle,
b – bottom, r – right, l – left,
c – centre. All photographs supplied
by Select Pictures except for:
Cover, 4tl, 6tl, 9, 10tl, 13, 14tl, 15,
20b, 21, 22b, 23ml, 24 all – Digital
Stock. 2tl, 5b, 19, 23tr –
Corbis/Royalty Free. 7, 10-11, 16tl,
22mr – Corbis. 8tl – Roger Vlitos.
20tl, 23br – John Foxx Images.

READING ABOUT

Hot and Cold

By Jim Pipe

Aladdin/Watts
London • Sydney

Hot and cold

Sonya and Greg go to see the animals at the park.

Some animals like hot places,
and some like cold places.

Greg and Sonya want to
see them all!

Hot

What is hot?

Today the sun is hot.

Sonya and Greg stand in the sun.

It makes them feel hot, too.

The sun is too hot for Sonya,
but not for the camels.

Camels live in a desert.
They stand in the sun all day.

Cold

What is cold?

Splash! That water is cold.

It makes Greg shiver.

But the seals love it!

If you jump in the sea on a hot day, it feels very cold!

Getting warm

What is warm?

Warm is a little hot.

Greg sits in the sun to get warm.

So does a crocodile!

In winter, this fox has fur to keep it warm. Greg and Sonya have winter coats to keep them warm.

Staying cool

What is cool?

Cool is a little cold.
When hippos get too warm,
they cool off in the water.

You can swim in a pool
to stay cool, too!

Fire

What is very hot?

Fire is very hot. Sonya and Greg eat hot dogs cooked on a fire.

When rocks get very, very hot, they melt. They glow like fire!

Ice

What is very cold?

When water gets very cold, it turns to ice. When ice gets warm, it turns to water!

The penguin house is very cold. Penguins live on the ice. They swim in the icy water. Brrrr!

Warm and damp

The rainforest hall is warm and damp.

Water drips from the trees and flowers. Bright birds call.

Soon Sonya and Greg feel warm and damp, too.

Wind

What is cool and dry?

The wind blows and makes
Sonya and Greg feel cool.
Inside, a fan makes a wind!

The wind makes things dry, too.

These towels are drying in
the wind.

Just right

What a day! The sun was hot,
then the penguin house was cold.

The rainforest was warm and damp,
then the wind was cool and dry.

Sonya and Greg sit under a tree.
Here it is not too hot and not
too cold.

It is just right!

Here are some words about heat.

Hot

Cold

Warm

Cool

Icy

Here are some hot and cold things.

Ice lolly

Desert

Fire

Sun

Pool

Can you write
a story with
these words?

Do you know?
When things get
hot or cold, they
change. Look what
happens to water!

When water
gets very cold,
it turns to ice
and snow.

When water gets
very hot, it boils.
It turns to steam.